LEVEL **1**

Hedgehogs

Mary Quattlebaum

NATIONAL GEOGRAPHIC

Washington, D.C.

To Arya, welcome to the world! —M.Q.

Published by National Geographic Partners, LLC, Washington, D.C. 20036.

Designed by Yay! Design

The author and publisher gratefully acknowledge the expert content review of this book by Mike McClure, general curator, the Maryland Zoo, and J. Jill Heatley, associate professor, Department of Small Animal Clinical Sciences, College of Veterinary Medicine & Biomedical Sciences, Texas A&M University, and the literacy review of this book by Mariam Jean Dreher, professor of reading education, University of Maryland, College Park.

Photo Credits

AS: Adobe Stock; ASP: Alamy Stock Photo; GI: Getty Images; SS: Shutterstock

Cover, KAMONRAT/SS; top border (throughout), Anvin Iwanicki/SS; vocabulary art (throughout), Linza/AS; 1, JL. Klein & ML. Hubert/Naturagency; 3, kisscsanad/AS; 4, praisaeng/AS; 6, ondrejprosicky/AS; 7 (UP), Oksana Schmidt/GI; 7 (LO), Eyal Bartov/ASP; 8, Mark Thiessen/NGP Staff; 9, Evgeniy/AS; 10, fotoparus/AS; 11, Film Studio Aves/GI; 12-13, fotomaster/AS; 14, Cyril Ruoso/Minden Pictures; 15, Paul Hobson/Nature Picture Library; 16, Anney/AS; 17, Ivan Gaddari/EyeEm/GI; 18, Henrik Larsson/AS; 19, torook/AS; 20 (UP), KAMONRAT/SS; 20 (CTR), vchphoto/AS; 20 (LO), Rico/AS; 21 (UP), imv/GI; 21 (CTR), Vickey Chauhan/SS; 21 (LO), Sergey Kivenko/AS; 22, Alain Le Toquin/Science Source; 23, edward-m/AS; 24-25, jonnysek/AS; 26-27, PerErik/AS; 28-29, Ingo Arndt/Minden Pictures; 30 (LE), nmelnychuk/AS; 30 (RT), jurra8/AS; 31 (UP LE), J. De Meester/Arco Images/ASP; 31 (UP RT), Henrik Larsson/AS; 31 (LO LE), Ingo Arndt/Minden Pictures; 31 (LO RT), Roger Allen Photography/ASP; 32 (UP LE), Anney/AS; 32 (UP RT), Alain Le Toquin/Science Source; 32 (LO LE), Oksana Schmidt/GI; 32 (LO RT), Ivan Gaddari/EyeEm/GI

Library of Congress Cataloging-in-Publication Data

Names: Quattlebaum, Mary, author.
Title: Hedgehogs / Mary Quattlebaum.
Description: Washington, DC: National Geographic Kids, 2020. | Series: National geographic readers | Audience: Ages 4-6 | Audience: Grades K-1
Identifiers: LCCN 2019051448 (print) | LCCN 2019051449 (ebook) | ISBN 9781426338304 (paperback) | ISBN 9781426338311 (library binding) | ISBN 9781426338328 (ebook) | ISBN 9781426338335 (ebook other)
Subjects: LCSH: Hedgehogs--Juvenile literature.
Classification: LCC QL737.E753 Q38 2020 (print) | LCC QL737.E753 (ebook) | DDC 599.33/2--dc23
LC record available at https://lccn.loc.gov/2019051448
LC ebook record available at https://lccn.loc.gov/2019051449

National Geographic supports K–12 educators with ELA Common Core Resources.
Visit natgeoed.org/commoncore for more information.

Printed in the United States of America
20/WOR/1

Table of Contents

What's a Hedgehog?

Is this a porcupine? Or a pinecone with a face?

No—it's a hedgehog!

Hedgehogs are small animals about the size of a guinea (GHIN-ee) pig. They have sharp spines on their head and back.

Where in the World?

Hedgehogs live on the ground in forests, fields, and deserts. They live in many parts of the world.

Hedgehogs live in parts of Africa, Asia, Europe, and the Middle East.

a European hedgehog in a field

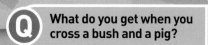

This hedgehog lives in the desert in Israel.

7

Sharp Spines

All hedgehogs have spines. Spines are hard, pointy hairs. They keep the hedgehog safe from animals that want to eat it. Foxes, badgers, owls, and hawks hunt hedgehogs.

A hedgehog spine has a sharp end that faces out.

Air pockets inside each spine make the spines light but strong.

When danger is near, a hedgehog curls into a ball. Its face and soft belly stay safe on the inside. The sharp spines stick out on the outside. The spines hurt animals that try to bite the hedgehog.

Parts of a Hedgehog

A hedgehog's body helps it find food and stay safe.

SPINES: Hard spines are made of the same stuff as human hair and nails.

CLAWS: Long claws help dig holes called burrows.

Hedgehog Points

BURROW: A hole dug in the ground that an animal uses as a home

SNOUT: An animal's nose and mouth that stick out from its face

SNOUT: A pointy snout sniffs out food. It pokes under leaves and around bushes and roots.

FUR: Fur covers the face, legs, feet, and belly. It protects the hedgehog's skin.

COLORING: A hedgehog's colors help it hide from animals that want to eat it. Its body blends in with the rocks and bushes around it. Hedgehogs can be brown, white, gray, or tan.

Hedgehog Homes

Some hedgehogs live in the country. They live in fields and close to farms.

Other hedgehogs live in cities and
towns. They live close to people.
They are found in yards, gardens,
and city parks.

a hedgehog just outside its burrow

Some hedgehogs dig a burrow for a home. Others make a nest on the ground with grass and leaves.

During the day, hedgehogs sleep in their homes. At night, they look for food. They are nocturnal (nok-TUR-nul).

Hedgehog Points

NOCTURNAL: Active at night

Dinnertime

What is a hedgehog's favorite food? Insects! They also munch on worms, snails, and slugs. Sometimes they eat small mice, spiders, lizards, fruit, and bird eggs.

Hedgehogs eat insects such as beetles.

6 COOL FACTS About Hedgehogs

1

A hedgehog can have as many as 6,000 spines.

2

Hedgehogs are strong swimmers.

3

Hedgehogs eat the hard bodies of insects. This helps a hedgehog clean its teeth.

4

The four-toed hedgehog in Africa has four toes on its back feet. All other hedgehogs have five.

5

Large ears help desert hedgehogs hear well and stay cool. Heat leaves their bodies through the thin skin of their ears.

6

Hedgehogs grunt and snuffle. They sound like pigs! Some people believe that's how they got the name "hedgehog."

At Rest

Some hedgehogs live in cold places. In the winter, they hibernate (HYE-bur-nate) in nests and burrows.

Hedgehog Points

HIBERNATE: To spend the cold winter months resting. An animal's body slows down when it hibernates.

Long-eared hedgehogs live
in hot areas like the desert.

Some hedgehogs live in hot places.
They sleep for many weeks during
the hot, dry summer. They rest
under plants or under the ground.

Hello, Hoglets!

Baby hedgehogs are called hoglets. Most females have four to seven hoglets at one time.

Newborn hoglets are pale pink with short, light-colored spines.

The babies are born with their eyes closed. Their spines are soft and short at first.

The hoglets drink their mother's milk. In a few weeks, their eyes open. They grow new spines that are long and stiff.

Q What do you get when you cross a hedgehog with a cucumber?

A A prickly pickle.

Their mother teaches them to find food. Soon, the hoglets can hunt without her help.

Helping Hedgehogs

Hedgehogs are helpful. They eat insects that harm plants. This keeps the plants that feed people and other animals safe.

People can help hedgehogs, too. They can plant bushes and hedges. These make safe places for hedgehogs to live.

People can also help hedgehogs by keeping hollow logs like this in yards and parks. Hollow logs are safe places for hedgehogs to make nests.

What in the World?

These pictures are up-close views of things in a hedgehog's world. Use the hints to figure out what's in the pictures. Answers are on page 31.

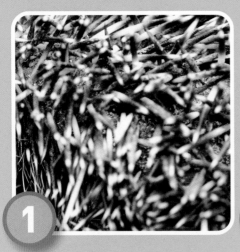

1

HINT: These protect a hedgehog.

2

HINT: This body part helps a hedgehog find food.

Word Bank

insect   hoglets   spines   burrow   claws   snout

3

HINT: These are used for digging.

4

HINT: A hedgehog's favorite food

5

HINT: Baby hedgehogs

6

HINT: A hedgehog's home in the ground

Answers: 1. spines, 2. snout, 3. claws, 4. insect, 5. hoglet, 6. burrow

BURROW: A hole dug in the ground that an animal uses as a home

HIBERNATE: To spend the cold winter months resting. An animal's body slows down when it hibernates.

NOCTURNAL: Active at night

SNOUT: An animal's nose and mouth that stick out from its face